Moonaby

Pronounced MOON-UH-BYE, like lullaby

Written & Illustrated
by
~ Kat Moore ~

Carnelian Moon
PUBLISHING

Published by Carnelian Moon Publishing Inc.
Ottawa, Canada

www.carnelianmoonpublishing.com

Cover design and interior artwork by Kat Moore
Interior layout by Simon Brimble

Paperback ISBN: 9 978-1-7376060-3-1 78-1-7376060-3-1
eBook ISNB: 978-1-7376060-2-4

Little one, to whom I speak, the sun
has gone onto tomorrow
Leaving you in midnight's arms to
carry you to morning's skies
It is time now for your dreams to
dance about you where the stars glow
Weaving tales of mystic places once
you close those sleepy eyes

The shadows fall about you as you
nuzzle deep into your bed
Through your window, in the heavens,
there shines a big balloon
Floating down, she comes to ease the
worries in your troubled head
Night's silver sun for you, little one,
and her name is Mama Moon

Mama Moon is here because she has
heard you've been afraid
When playtime stops, bedtime starts,
and you've said all of your prayers
When the lights are dimmed and you
are left alone in evening's shade
You sometimes see and hear things
that you think are really there

Those shadows on the wall sometimes
may look a little strange
Faces form and figures move and
dance within the night
Mama Moon says you have magic that
can make those shadows change
Your own mind can bring new visions,
happy pictures to your sight

Just imagine funny people, silly things,
and pleasant places
Butterflies and rainbows, fields of
daisies in the sun
Soon you will forget all of the dark
land's scary faces
You will learn that watching shadows
can become a game of fun

"What's that," you say? You hear
something go bumping in the night?
A moaning, creaky-sounding thing or
footsteps on the floor?
Mama Moon knows to hear these
things may give a child a fright
So listen closely, little one, you need
not worry anymore

Many things can bring these sounds to
life, like the wind's song in the trees
Shutters swing upon their hinges,
thunder quakes, a nightbird calls
The same magic that you use to tame
the shadows that you see
Can calm the fear of the noises you
hear the next time nighttime falls

Little one, you are so young, this world
so vast and wild
But you've a certain specialness as
only a little one could
Your time on earth a labyrinth through
which you wander, child
With its many traps to trip you and its
watchers in the wood

Now stay within the starlight where
Mama Moon has been your guide
These words will keep you in her care,
for she must now move on
To brighten other darkened skies, to
sing with wolves and turn the tides
An orb in endless wandering, tail-
chaser of the dawn

~ MOONABY ~

Shadowtime, I do not fear you
No monsters here
No goblins prowl
No banshees scream
I take away my faith in you
And in your place spring forth colors
Kaleidoscopes
Bold spectrums
Blazing hues dissolve the barren black
Fairy folk, come sit beside me
All unicorns
All enchantment
All fawns and elfin kings
Rejoice within my dreams now
Take all of my imaginings and send them
Soaring in the wind
Crystal castles
Jade-green forests
Skies of lapis-blue
The borders of your land are infinite
My visits with you are timeless
I shall slip into my imaginings
Slumber deep within my dreams now
With the laughter
With the singing
With the dancing
With the echoes of a world newly born to me
Beneath the haloed moon

(Never quite)

~ THE END ~

Dedication

This book is lovingly dedicated to Fraser and its incredible staff, especially my son Aidan's wonderful therapist, Keary. They have been instrumental in Aidan's growth and mental well-being, and they have been a lifeline to me as a single mom of a Special Needs child. Fraser helps individuals navigate autism, mental health, and diverse intellectual, emotional, and physical needs at every stage of life. The nonprofit provides education, employment, healthcare, and housing to help clients thrive. It is with much gratitude that I am donating 10% of net proceeds from this book to Fraser. Visit www.fraser.org to learn more.

About the Author

Kat is an author-illustrator, singer-songwriter, and activist. She created Katseye Innovative in early 2020 to give to the world through her writing, art, music, and activism. Her first project was her song "Broken Moon" and its video that she released in November, 2020 to raise funds and awareness for gun safety and mental health. Moonaby is Kat's first children's book and the project's philanthropic focus is on autism, in honor of her amazing son Aidan who is on the Autism Spectrum. She continues to work on her various creative projects and resides in Minnetonka, Minnesota with Aidan and Garfield, their lovable, mischievous feline companion. www.katseyeinnovative.com

Kat Moore (Lucas Botz Photography, 2019).

Kat & Aidan's Story

Kat wrote Moonaby in 1992, twelve years before she welcomed Aidan into the world. Born in 2004, Aidan won the hearts of those around him with his sweet and funny personality

Kat and Aidan in 2010 (LimeSmile Images, 2010).

and his quick and clever mind. At the age of six, Aidan was diagnosed with autism and severe ADHD. Over the years, Kat has worked with Aidan's healthcare professionals and educators to learn all that she can to be Aidan's advocate and help him navigate life on the Autism Spectrum. She couldn't be prouder of how hard Aidan has worked throughout the years to become the amazing young man he is today!

Although life's twists and turns brought about many changes and moves in the early years, Kat and Aidan have been living most happily together in the Minnetonka, Minnesota area since 2015. Aidan's wish for having a Ginger Tabby of his own came true in 2016 when they rescued their feline friend, Garfield. Kat's writing, art, and singing + Aidan's video gaming and vibing with his friends + Garfield's crazy, cuddly ways = a home ever and always filled with music, laughter, and love.

Kat and Aiden in 2021 (Moore, 2021).

Meet Garfield

Garfield in the Christmas tree (Moore, 2020).

Meow meow meow meow meow, Garfield meow meow meow. Meow meow September meow 2016, meow meow meow meow December meow meow. Meow meow meow Kat and Aidan, meow meow Minnetonka, Minnesota. Meow, Garfield meow meow meow!

CPSIA information can be obtained
at www.ICGtesting.com
Printed in the USA
BVHW020622210821
614946BV00016B/551